To Fly With The
SWALLOWS
A Story of Old California

To Fly With The
SWALLOWS
A Story of Old California

by Dana Catharine de Ruiz
Alex Haley, General Editor

Illustrations by Debbe Heller

STECK-VAUGHN
C O M P A N Y
ELEMENTARY • SECONDARY • ADULT • LIBRARY

Published by Steck-Vaughn Company.

Text, illustrations and cover art copyright © 1993 by
Dialogue Systems, Inc., 627 Broadway, New York,
New York 10012. All rights reserved.

Cover art by Mary Beth Schwark

Printed in the United States of America
2 3 4 5 6 7 8 9 0 LB 00 99 98 97

Library of Congress Cataloging-in-Publication Data

De Ruiz, Dana Catharine, 1945–
    To fly with the swallows : a story of old California / Dana
Catharine de Ruiz : illustrator, Debbe Heller.
        p.   cm. — (Stories of America)
    Summary: A biography of the woman who became
California's first native-born nun, describing a life that
spanned the transitional period from Spanish rule to
American statehood.
        ISBN 0-8114-7234-5. — ISBN 0-8114-8074-7 (pbk.)
        1. Argüello y Morago, María de Concepción, d. 1857—
Juvenile literature. 2. Nuns—California—Biography—
Juvenile literature. [1. Argüello y Morago, María de
Concepción, d. 1857. 2. Nuns. 3. California—
History.] I. Heller, Debbe, ill. II. Title. III. Series.
BX4705.A677D4   1993
979.4'04'092—dc20
[B]   92-14416
                                                           CIP
                                                            AC

ISBN 0-8114-7234-5 (Hardcover)

ISBN 0-8114-8074-7 (Softcover)

Introduction
by Alex Haley, General Editor

Spanish colonial history is often ignored when we study the history of our nation. The focus is always on the English and the Thirteen Colonies. But there were other European colonies in America before the English, and most of them were Spanish.

The Spanish stamp was placed not only on Mexico and the countries farther south in Central and South America but on a large part of what is now the United States as well. The Carolinas, Florida, Georgia, Mississippi, Louisiana, Texas, Colorado, Arizona, and California all began their colonial history with Spanish explorers and, in most cases, Spanish settlers.

Other books in this series tell the story of Spanish exploration and settlement. *To Fly with the Swallows* tells a different story. It provides a glimpse of Spanish life in colonial America. It also tells the story of how a young girl built a new dream from the ashes of an old one.

Paz y bien, hermanos

Contents

Part One
1806

1

The End of the World

Concha stirred in her bed as the morning birds chirped and sang. The sunlight filtered in through the cracks in the wooden shutters. It was April of 1806. Fifteen-year-old Concha—María de la Concepción Marcela Argüello y Moraga—stretched out her arms and yawned. She climbed out of bed carefully so as not to disturb the sleep of her little sisters. She smoothed the dark curls from Ana Paula's forehead and kissed Gertrudis's damp brow.

There were 15 Argüello children. Two were no longer at home. But still there was not much room, so Concha shared a room and a bed with two of her sisters. Even though their father was *comandante*—commander—of the presidio of

Yerba Buena, the Argüello house was not much grander than its neighbors.

Once out of bed, Concha ran softly to the little window cut into the thick adobe wall. She threw open the shutters and leaned so far out that her feet were no longer touching the floor. Swinging her feet back and forth reminded her of being a little girl in a big chair, unable to reach the floor. She smothered a laugh with her hand.

From her window, Concha could see over the thatched roofs of the other houses of the presidio to the bay. This was the border of Alta California, the northernmost point of the Spanish Empire in North America. This was the end of the world, she thought. There was the Pacific Ocean. Its blue waters, stretching endlessly west, carried frail ships to faraway places—Japan and China and Russia! But that was another world away.

Concha looked down on the nearby homes of the soldiers of her father's command. They and their families lived beneath the thatched roofs of the presidio houses. The soldiers in Yerba Buena were there to protect Spain's claim to this land. The British and French were interested in this land. So were the Russians.

Right next door to Concha's house, in the center of the presidio, was the church. It was the center of their lives as well.

Concha could see the sun as it rose over San Francisco Bay. The bay was named by the Spanish for St. Francis. Concha thought that St. Francis would have been pleased. The bay area was a wonderful place for animals, and the saint had loved animals greatly.

She could see small groups of deer coming down through the woodlands to look for food along the water's edge. Playful sea otters romped and frolicked in the bay. Concha knew that their fur was very valuable and that many traders would come to Yerba Buena if the government of Spain allowed it. But it did not.

Spain did not even encourage visitors from other countries. It had been a very long time since any ship had sailed into the bay. This was partly because of Spanish policy, but mostly it was because Alta California was such a long way from Europe or Asia.

Concha looked up. The *golondrinas*—the swallows that had returned barely two weeks ago—were joyfully diving and swooping above the water. How graceful they were!

Oh! To be like the swallows! Free and able

to fly away to distant lands when they were tired of the too quiet life of Alta California! Perhaps they had flown to Mexico City. Perhaps they had nestled in the eaves of the houses of her cousins who dressed in fine silks and danced the elegant new European dance steps. How long would it take the swallows to fly to Mexico City? To travel overland, Concha knew, would take close to eight months.

Concha uncovered the jug of water and poured it into the basin. As she splashed water on her face, she thought of the many compliments that had been paid her. Because of her beauty and lively spirit, she had already received several proposals of marriage. And turned them all down.

Many of her friends were married at fifteen, so her refusals were not because she was too young. Her suitors had been young men of good character with large ranches to their names, so her reasons for not marrying were not because the suitors were unworthy. Her parents did not force her to consider marriage. They were not unhappy that she chose to remain with them, for they loved her very dearly and wished only her happiness.

Concha patted her face dry. No, she did not

wish to marry and remain in Yerba Buena. She arranged her long, black hair into a neat braid and pulled on a blouse and a muslin skirt. As she belted her skirt with a red sash, she danced around the room.

No, she thought, I would rather travel like the swallows and see the places they have seen, the places I have read about in the books the padres have given me. She danced quietly so as not to waken Mamá.

Mamá! If I hurry, she thought, I can bring her a cup of chocolate before she gets up. I know she must be lonely with Papá away in Monterey visiting Governor Arrillaga. The chocolate will cheer her.

Concha ran along the hard-packed earth floors of the little house. The sun coming through the windows shone brilliantly off the whitewashed walls. When she passed the family altar, its tallow candles flickering, she quickly crossed herself.

She continued running out to the *ramada*—the vine-covered enclosure where the cooking was done. Already the pungent smell of woodsmoke mingled with the homely smell of beans bubbling in the great clay cooking pot. Concha could hear the slap, slap, slap, of the

Indian servant's hands as she prepared the cornmeal for the breakfast tortillas.

Another servant was cooking chocolate on the oven. She knelt by the oven, fanning its fire with a straw fan. Then she stood to beat the chocolate to a fine froth. Concha held up a small clay cup as the Indian woman filled it with steaming chocolate. Then Concha covered it with a little cloth that she herself had embroidered, put it on a tray, and carried it to Mamá.

¡Conchita, muchas gracias!

Her mother took the chocolate and handed over the two youngest members of the Argüello family to Concha. They were the little ones who still slept with Mamá. Ay, thought Concha, I am called "little Concha" but I have to care for my little brother and sister as if I were grown and they were my own children! With one strong arm she scooped the baby up, and with the other she took the toddler by the hand.

Concha took the little ones out to the central patio of the presidio, scuffing her shoes in the thick dust as she went. All the little houses were built around this patio, and most family activities took place here.

Impulsively, Concha tickled the baby to make him giggle and kissed his round little face.

She pretended that the two of them were at the fanciest ball in Mexico City. No, the fanciest ball in Madrid, and they were dressed in elegant clothes—the baby in a handsome military uniform and she, Concha, in the finest of silks. She imagined her dress making a wonderful swishy sound as they danced around the floor. All eyes were on them—the handsomest couple on the dance floor!

She danced around and around the patio, the baby chortling happily.

The patio was brilliant with sunlight. The sweet scent of the *Rosa de Castilla*, which climbed up the houses of the presidio, filled the morning air. Concha handed the baby over to a servant and called to her little sisters to bring the basket with her embroidery.

Concha had been sewing since she was seven years old, and many of the fine linens of their household had been embroidered by her hand. Now the little ones sat at her feet and learned from her how to thread their needles and sew.

Girls from the other presidio families came out with their younger brothers and sisters.

¡Hola! ¿Cómo estás?
¡Bien! Gracias.

They all asked politely after each other and their families although everyone knew everyone else as well as if they had grown up in the same house. It seemed like one enormous family.

After the pleasantries of the morning and what little news there might be had been shared, the girls and young women settled down to their tasks. The older boys and young men would already be out on horseback, overseeing the field work of the Indians.

The sounds of the little ones playing and laughing were joined by the calls of the gulls flying overhead. When the children's voices hushed every now and then, Concha could hear the beating of the gulls' wings against the sea air.

¡Hay un barco! ¡Un barco! ¡Don Luis! ¡Que venga Don Luis!

Concha jumped up, spilling the contents of her basket, the embroidery threads rolling into the dust. A ship! They were calling her brother because a ship had been sighted! A ship! Concha ran with the other girls to the presidio wall. There hadn't been a ship in ages!

The girls leaned as far as they could, straining to see the speck that moved toward them on the horizon. Each wanted to be the first to say where it came from, but it was still too far away to make out its flag.

Oh! thought Concha, this ship, wherever it comes from, will surely bring excitement and adventure! Perhaps it is British like the ship of Señor Vancouver. There was so much feasting and dancing when that ship came that people still talked about the visit although it was over thirteen years ago.

Concha kicked her feet excitedly against the presidio wall. Even though I was a baby, I was brought to all the parties, Concha recalled. I was so little I would not even remember it, if the people did not tell so many stories about it. There was a formal dance aboard ship and beautiful fireworks!

Concha left her little brothers and sisters with her friends. Her brother would have to go to meet the ship since he was acting *comandante* while their father was away. She must go help him dress. She ran back to the house and shook out Luis's dress sarape. It was a deep wine-red color, and she folded it carefully over Luis's shoulder, telling him how elegant he looked. She reached up and kissed his cheek.

Luis quickly pulled on his best embroidered deerskin boots. The other soldiers of the presidio waited outside, their horses stamping their hooves and causing little clouds of dust to billow up. The horses whickered and blew air through their velvety nostrils.

Concha held the silver-banded bridle of Luis's horse, rubbing the horse's muzzle gently to calm him. She knew as much about horses as any man there. She had been riding since she was six years old. She wanted very much to ride down to the shore with the men, but she didn't even think of asking. She knew it would be considered improper for a woman.

As Luis mounted his horse, Concha asked him to be sure to invite the travelers back for refreshments. Even though official policy discouraged foreigners from coming to Alta California, the people of California were well-known for their hospitality. Mamá stood in the doorway and nodded, smiling to Luis. She encouraged him to welcome them on behalf of his father and the presidio. Luis and the other young men wheeled their horses round and galloped off.

2

Strands Woven Together

Concha ran to join her friends at the presidio wall. The small ship had two tall masts from which hung square sails. Soon after the ship dropped anchor, some men began rowing a tiny boat toward shore.

Again, the girls tried to guess where the ship came from but none of them could recognize the strange flag it bore.

The men in the rowboat reached the shore, and the meeting began. Everyone gathered on the beach looked very small and far away, but even from this distance, the girls could see them waving and using hand signals. What could all those wild gestures mean? What could they be saying?

Then, suddenly, one of the young men dug his spurs into his horse's side and came galloping back up to the presidio. The girls looked at each other, their dark eyes wide in amazement. Why was he leaving? Was there danger? Had he come to get help? What was the matter?

In minutes, the young man and his horse came clattering into the patio. "Padre Uria! Padre Uria!" he called as he jumped from his horse to look for the Franciscan priest. He told everyone who would listen—which was *everyone*—that the strangers were Russians. Their ship was called the *Juno,* and no one on it spoke Spanish. Luckily, one of them spoke Latin. That was why Padre Uria was needed.

Padre Uria, like every other Catholic priest at the time, spoke Latin. The old padre came out of the church, hoisted up his long gray robes, and climbed into the saddle of his horse. Off the horse trotted, down to the bay after the young messenger.

¿Rusos? Russians? What can they be like? Concha knew that for over two years the arrival of the first Russian around-the-world expedition had been expected. Might this small ship be part of that expedition? If so, would the other

ships known to be part of that expedition, the *Nadeschda* and the *Neva*, soon follow? Spain had sent orders to welcome these ships.

But what if they were traders interested in the pelts of the sea otters? Spain had forbidden trade. There could be trouble. Concha gathered her little brothers and sisters and ran back to the house to tell Mamá. If she hurried, she would have time to change into a more suitable dress to welcome the strangers.

Soon the hoofbeats of the approaching horses could be heard as the men returned with their guests. Concha's heart pounded in her chest as she sat waiting with her family.

Mamá was dressed beautifully and sat cross-legged on a platform a few inches off the floor. Her children sat beside her.

Concha could hardly contain herself. She wanted to peer out the window to see these exciting and very foreign visitors. She could hear the creaking of the big leather saddles and the jangle of the bridles as the riders dismounted. Then she heard footsteps and the familiar voice of her brother as he led the visitors toward the house.

Concha wanted to jump up and run to the

door to be the first to welcome them. But she knew that for a *comandante's* daughter, that would not be seemly. She must represent Spain and her family well. She would remain seated.

Concha looked up from under her long dark lashes as her brother brought his guests before his family. Two of the men were introduced. They were the two most important guests—Count Nikolai Petrovich Rezanov, the commander of the expedition, and a German named Von Langsdorff, the ship's doctor and its Latin scholar.

Mamá welcomed them.

Concha felt the color rise in her cheeks as she realized that these men were staring at her. She had been told many times before that she was beautiful, but it was something different to be noticed by world travelers such as these men must be. The tall, pale commander captured her attention from the start. Count Rezanov wore a green military uniform. Looking back at him, Concha realized that—world traveler though he be—she too had made quite an impression on him.

The younger children went to help Mamá bring chocolate and *panecillos*—little cakes—to their guests, while Luis and Concha were left to entertain them.

Concha thought how simple their house must appear to these men. In a rush to impress them, she told them of the Argüello Rancho that was not too far away. There, the Argüellos had much more land. And the rancho house was roomier and grander than this. But we Argüellos live in Yerba Buena, she explained, for convenience's sake since Father is *comandante* here. If they would care to see the rancho, Luis would arrange to take them for a visit.

Luis suggested that they might hunt partridge on their visit. That would surely be appealing to men who had been on board ship for such a long time.

While Luis was arranging plans for the visit, Concha was thinking that she might also get him to organize a *baile*—a dance—for the evening. Not a formal European dance, but a simple party such as they were accustomed to having at the presidio. Concha took Luis by the shoulder and whispered her idea in his ear. And, she said, find out more about this man, the Count—he is very interesting.

The day of the *baile* arrived. Concha and her

friends decorated the long *sala*—main room—of the Argüello house, while the servants moved the rough-hewn furniture and swept the hard-packed floor.

The delicious smells of beef and beans wafted in from the *ramada*. Little cakes were being prepared. There would be plenty of simple but good fare.

Concha had learned that the men from the *Juno* had come from Sitka, Russia's colony in Alaska. The Sitka colony was in need of fresh food supplies. In fact, that is why Rezanov had come south to Yerba Buena. But permission for that would have to wait for Papá's return and Governor Arrillaga's consent. In the meantime, she felt sure that the everyday food of the presidio would seem like a feast to the Russians.

The musicians arrived with guitars and violins. The rustle of silks announced the arrival of the guests. Rafaela Sal, Luis's betrothed, arrived with her startlingly red hair beautifully arranged. Carolina Ximeno and Herminia Lopez covered their excited faces, unfolding the *abanicos*—fans—that were brought from Spain long ago by their mothers and grandmothers.

The music began. Two couples started the

borrego, which was a popular dance at the time. Spanish couples sang and danced and stamped their feet, then taught their Russian guests the steps. The Russians joined in. Von Langsdorff jumped up and spoke to the musicians. Then he modeled the steps of yet another dance. Within minutes, most everyone was dancing along with him.

Concha fluttered her fan as Count Rezanov approached her for a dance. The Count was very polite and danced with every lady in the room, even Mamá. But he returned over and over again to dance with Concha. He seemed enchanted with the warm hospitality of the Argüello family. But even more than that, he seemed enchanted with Concha herself.

Count Rezanov knew French, which is not too different from Spanish, so he was able to pick up enough Spanish so the two could converse. While they danced around the *sala,* Concha agreed to teach Rezanov proper Spanish if he would tell her about the exotic life of St. Petersburg, where the Czar held court in Russia.

At evening's end, when the last of the guests had said their goodbyes and gone, Concha stood in the doorway and looked up into the night sky.

It was rich with silver stars shining against a velvety midnight-blue background. Concha looked and thought about the wide world the stars shone down upon. It was a world that seemed so much richer and wider than it had just a few days before. A world that suddenly had Yerba Buena at its center.

Every day, Concha and her family entertained their Russian guests in hunting parties or dances or with a simple cup of steaming chocolate to start the day. And every day, Count Nikolai Rezanov, who had traveled nearly around the world, found himself more and more enchanted by young Concha, who had never left Alta California.

Nikolai knew that Concha might be useful to him. She was the favorite of both her father, the *comandante,* and of Governor Arrillaga. But his interest in her went beyond her possible usefulness to him. Concha was so different from any other woman he had ever known. She was a miracle of youth, intelligence, and beauty.

As they got to know each other more and more, Nikolai's interest was replaced by a growing affection. He began to think less of her usefulness to him and more of how rich life would be with her at his side.

23

And every day, Concha found herself more and more interested in Nikolai Rezanov. The world he spoke of seemed to her like a dream come true. It seemed like a stage where she could act out all the exciting and wonderful scenes she had always imagined. The life she imagined in St. Petersburg seemed to have the brilliance of the sun, while life at the presidio seemed very dull and lost in the shadows by comparison.

One afternoon, Concha and Nikolai were seated on a bench in the central patio. The patio was crowded with people. Little children played nearby. The sailors of the *Juno* and the young soldiers of the presidio huddled together in small groups. They gossiped and exchanged information using few words and many gestures.

Nikolai and Concha were talking, of all things, about the weather. The climate in St. Petersburg, Nikolai explained, was very severe. It might be made more pleasant, he continued softly, if Concha were to join him there. Would she consent to marry him?

Concha colored deeply, and whispered that in Alta California, one did not speak of these things to a young woman. One must ask her father. But . . . yes!

The happy news brought tears and confusion to the Argüello family. Papá had returned. He thought highly enough of Rezanov to approve his request for supplies, but this was another matter entirely. Concha to marry a foreigner and a non-Catholic one at that? *¡Nunca!* Never! Why, Russia was half the world away! They would never see her again. This could never be permitted.

Papá and Mamá went without sleep, arguing with Concha to give up this plan. Concha listened, but refused to change her mind or her heart. She was sent to the priests for advice. She knew that if the priests would give permission, her parents would, too, no matter how sad they might be at losing her.

But the priests were puzzled by the problem. Rezanov was not a Catholic, but he was a Christian. This was clearly a matter for the head of the Catholic Church to decide. Rezanov must go to Rome and ask permission of the Catholic Pope. Then he must ask permission of the King of Spain. If he would do these things, then the priests and the Argüellos would give their permission for the wedding to take place.

The day came for Nikolai Rezanov and the crew of the *Juno* to leave the presidio. He could not take Concha with him as his bride. But he would begin the journey that would give him permission to marry her. It would take at least two years for him to travel to Russia for the Czar's permission, which he was sure of, then to Italy for the Pope's, and on to Spain for the King's, and then, finally, back to Alta California.

Great tears welled up in Concha's eyes. Nikolai felt a deep sadness at parting from his young love but promised to write from every port.

On Wednesday, May 21, with the hold stored with supplies, the *Juno* made ready to weigh anchor. The Russians had spent six delightful weeks in the fertile and beautiful bay area. Now it was time to leave.

On the beach, the crew members bade farewell to the kind and hospitable *Californios.* In pledge of her love, Concha gave Nikolai her gold locket. Its cover was enameled in black and bore a cross of tiny seed pearls. Inside the locket were strands of hair woven together, hers and his.

Concha and her family stood on the beach waving goodbye until the square sails of the little ship were nothing more than specks on the horizon. When all sign of the brig had disappeared, Concha wrapped her shawl around her

shoulders and hugged herself. She reached for the plump hand of little Gertrudis. Together they returned slowly to the presidio and home.

Life would seem very dull without the constant company of the exotic visitors from the north. Already it seemed very quiet and lonely without the deep Russian voices harmonizing with the music of the Spanish.

When she reached home, Concha knelt at the family altar. The light of the tallow candles flickered over the statue of the Virgin Mary. Concha prayed for a safe voyage and a speedy return for Nikolai. Then she searched for her embroidery. She and Nikolai would have to wait for their life together, but she would begin to make preparations for that life now.

Part Two

1842

3

Let Us Begin

An anxious figure came running up to the heavy wooden door of a sleepy house in Santa Barbara. It was early morning, before the sun had even come up—too early for visitors. The caller began yanking the bell rope with great energy. The sudden clanging startled even the roosters from their sleep. They flapped their wings with annoyance and cried out to the morning.

As soon as the sound of the bell first disturbed the morning calm, Concha had jumped out of bed. She knew the call was for her. Such calls—whether they came in the middle of the night or in the early morning or during meal-

31

times—were always for her. They were the unexpected calls of people whose loved ones or neighbors were sick or dying or giving birth.

Concha pulled on a plain gray dress. It was made of the same cloth and of the same style as the robes of the Franciscan missionaries. Concha wore it because long ago she had taken vows to live simply in the spirit of St. Francis.

Rushing to get ready, she splashed water on her still lovely face. Doña Concha was now over fifty years old. She quickly brushed out her long, dark hair. As she reached into her small keepsake box for her hairpins, her fingers came upon the little gold and enamel locket she had given Nikolai Rezanov thirty-six years before.

He had never returned from Russia. At first, she had received his letters. Then, nothing. For over five years she waited to learn what had become of him. Finally, a ship brought a young Russian officer to her with terrible news. Nikolai had died in Siberia.

He had been thrown from his horse into the icy waters of the Allach Juni River. His friends rescued him from the river and covered him with dry blankets. But they could do little else. Nikolai became ill and feverish before they could reach shelter and the warmth of a fire.

Afterwards, he forced himself to continue the long overland journey across Siberia. His condition worsened until he became so ill that he fell unconscious from his horse.

His friends refused to allow him to continue. Instead, they brought him to the governor's house in Krasnoiarsk to recover. They cared for him as best they could, but it was too late. There, Nikolai died.

His last words had been of Concha. The young officer who brought the news had told her this as he handed her the locket.

The news had shattered Concha. For a long time, she believed that Nikolai was the sole purpose of her life. She believed that without him, she had no reason to go on living. But, gradually, she found a new purpose in life. She would serve the poor. She would assist those who needed help because they were sick or lacked food and teach those who wanted to learn.

Now, every day brought a new reason for living—teaching the little ones, healing and comforting the sick, helping to bring a new baby into the world. And some days brought callers who rang her bell in the pre-dawn darkness because someone was dying.

Paz y bien, hermana. Peace, my sister. Con-

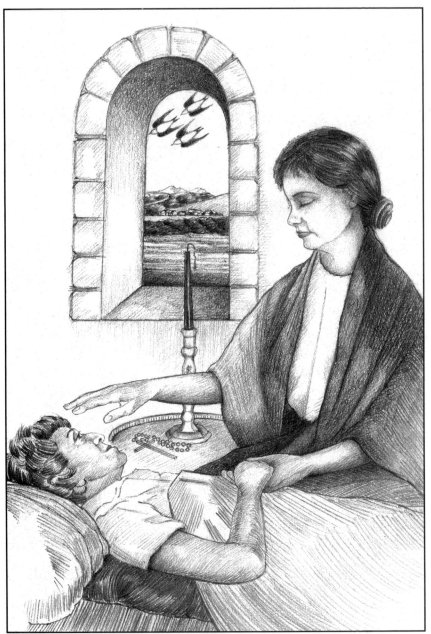

cha greeted the old woman who lay on her deathbed. She sat by her side, whispering prayers and holding her pale wrinkled hand until the old woman breathed her last. Concha took two large heavy coins and placed them on the old woman's eyelids.

Because Concha had longed for her own death, she must have thought it strange to be so often present at the deaths of others. Perhaps she remembered her visit to Bishop García Diego earlier that year. She had gone to complain of her own lost life.

The bishop was a kindly man and listened sympathetically. He agreed that the death of Nikolai had been a tragedy, but that was many years ago.

Then Bishop García Diego reminded her that she had promised to follow the example of St. Francis. There is more to this than wearing a simple dress and saying prayers. There are also St. Francis's teachings and his beliefs.

Everyone knew the story of how St. Francis began each day. He greeted every morning by saying, "Let us begin." He did this whether he was discouraged or not. "Let us begin." It was time for Concha to begin again. And so she did.

Concha began to arrange and dress the

body of the old woman. In the now quiet hands, Concha entwined a rosary and gently bent to kiss her forehead. *"Vaya con Dios,"* she said. Go with God.

Soon, all the friends and relatives would come to pay their respects. Concha saw to it that all the candlesticks in the house were placed at the head and foot of the body. She sliced an onion and placed it on a little plate under the table where the body lay. This was to absorb any bad odors in the air.

Indian servants brought in armloads of *nardos*—the tuberose flower—with their heavy sweet scent. Concha cut fancy paper frills to go around the candles. People would be coming all day and staying to pray all night, so there must be many candles. Some of the servants stood around the room, singing the prayers that the mission fathers had taught them years ago.

Concha saw to it that food was prepared for all the people who would come. Some would come from far away, so there must be plenty of meat to give energy to those who arrived tired from their travels. There must be hot drinks to give strength and cool lemonade with lots of sugar to restore the sad ones.

When all was in order, Concha knelt among

the flowers and said her prayers and then her goodbyes.

The messenger who had called for her in the morning accompanied her back home, holding her arm in the darkness that was lit only by the star-filled sky.

Tomorrow she would leave the house early. She was going to visit her friends, the Soberanes family. It was a journey of more than a hundred miles on horseback out to their rancho. It would be good to rest before such a long trip.

4

The Fullness of Life

Concha's legs and back ached. This was her second day of travel on horseback. It was two days of hard riding from Santa Barbara to reach La Soledad, the rancho of the Soberanes family. She and her servant had stayed the night with other friends, but they had to be on their way early again this morning. Concha knew that a new baby was expected at La Soledad, and babies don't wait.

It was not too hard to leave the rancho where they had just spent the night. Although the ranchero and his wife were kind and generous, their beds had been made of rough hide. And there had been fleas.

As Concha traveled north toward the Salinas River valley, she could see the round, grassy hills that filled the valley plain. The Gabilan mountain range was to the east of the river. Now it was just beginning to turn green with the summer's growth. From here on, Concha and her servant would probably not see another person until they reached their destination.

Towards evening, Concha pulled her cloak about her gray homespun dress. The sun was going down over the valley, and it was beginning to grow cool. She pulled her small sturdy horse to a stop. She and her servant had traveled over fifty miles this day.

The early evening sun shone through the tall grasses. There grew the yellow mustard plants in abundance and the small, daisy-like camomile. By the riverbank grew the mint *yerba buena*—the good herb—the name of the place where she had been born. But that was so long ago. She felt now that she was an entirely different person from the Concha who had lived at Yerba Buena.

Concha dismounted with the help of her servant. Although she ached, the help was given more out of respect than necessity. Concha was a strong woman and had already outlasted sev-

eral servants who were a great deal younger than she.

Together, Concha and her servant began gathering great armfuls of the healing herbs. Mint for the stomach, camomile for colic, mustard for aches and pains. Perhaps she would use some of this mustard for herself after this trip!

It had been a long time since she had seen the Soberanes family. She was sure they would need healing of some sort.

As she worked, an eerie sound rose from the river banks. Concha stood up, remembering that this same moaning of the wind through the willow branches had given name to this place— La Soledad. The first missionaries had heard the haunting, lonely sound and named their mission for Our Lady of Solitude. Concha called this place "the valley of the moaning winds."

As she packed away the precious herbs, Concha thought of the beautifully illustrated pages of the herbal book she had learned from. There was only one volume to serve the whole community, so it had come to her worn, old, and in tatters. But it was still beautiful.

The book was a treasure because there were no schools of any kind, nor were there any doctors to learn from. What knowledge she had came from a lifetime of experience in a large family—where there was always a birth or a death or healing of some kind to attend to—and from the herbal book. She had spent many long hours poring over it, learning the healing properties of plants and grasses. From the Indians, she had learned to use native flowers and tree bark as remedies.

On the last leg of her journey, Concha could now see the Soberanes ranch house high on a knoll overlooking the valley. She was very glad to see the long, low whitewashed house of sun-baked adobe brick. Tired and dusty from the long ride, she looked forward to a refreshing bath in the stream nearby.

As she drew closer, shouts of *"¡Allí viene Doña Concha! ¡Bienvenida!"* went up from the Soberanes family, young and old, master and servant.

The *aguador* let down with a splash his yoke that supported two pails of water. The *arrieros* in the corral in front of the house left the horses and climbed over the fence to greet her.

A young Indian boy ran up to help her dismount, while another came to take care of her horse.

Concha was warmly welcomed by everyone from Don Feliciano himself down to the youngest servant with warm *abrazos*—bearhugs of greeting. She always had time for everyone, whether in friendship, healing, or teaching. And she had brought those special little candies—*dulces*—with her from Santa Barbara for the little ones who had learned their lessons well.

Amidst the excited, affectionate cries of the children, she was led to a chair on the porch. The chair was built of rough wood and covered with hide, but it felt comfortable after two days in the saddle.

A little girl ran up with a cup of fresh, cool lemonade. While Concha sipped, the questions began to fly back and forth. The Soberanes family hadn't had any visitors in a long time, and they were hungry for news about their friends and relatives in the city.

How was the journey? Did you go to the big wedding? What was the fiesta like? Who was there? Were there many pretty dresses? Doña Concha had questions of her own. How was everyone here? Were the little ones learning from their lessons? Had she arrived in time for the birth of the newest baby?

After only a few minutes of rest, Doña Concha was hurried into the house by the Soberanes women—one giving her arm in support, another with her arm around Doña Concha. The little ones tagged along, tugging at her skirts until they were sent off to play in the twilight.

The little room she entered was dimly lit by the flickering light of a tallow candle. The young woman lying on the cowhide bed looked up and smiled. Doña Concha's skill as a midwife was well-known throughout the valley. The mother-to-be would now deliver her baby with the best help available.

The arrival of a new baby was always cause for a fiesta. The musicians had arrived and everyone was dancing when Concha brought in the newest member of the Soberanes family. She held him up for all to see.

The baby was dressed in clothes that Concha had lovingly embroidered to welcome this little one. She handed the baby over to one of the servants and looked with happiness at the scene before her. Young and old danced together on the simple, packed-earth floor of the rancho. Above the dancers flew the swallows, diving and swooping in the evening light.

Concha remembered that once she had wanted to be like the swallows so she could fly away to other lands and learn the fullness of life. She had not been able to fly away as she had once wanted so much to do. But, like the swallows, she had found joy and fulfillment.

Epilogue

Doña Concha's life spanned three entirely different periods of California history. She was born during the last days of Spanish mission rule and, as the daughter of the acting Governor, Don José Darío Argüello, she was an active participant in the life of the Spanish nobility in San Francisco and Monterey. She lived through the changing period of Mexican independence from Spain, and spent the last seven years of her life under the flag of the United States.

Doña Concha began her life of teaching, healing, and midwifery during California's last chaotic days as part of Mexico. The war with the United States, the Gold Rush, and streams of new settlers pouring in under a practically non-existent government contributed to the confusion.

Doña Concha became perhaps the most beloved woman of her time in California. Her good works took her from the elegance of the governor's mansion to the poorest of adobe huts. At a time when there was much discrimination, Doña Concha ministered to everyone who needed help, regardless of race, religion, or economic status. She provided comfort and stability in a time of chaos.

At age sixty, Doña Concha entered the first convent in California, in Santa Catalina. As California's first nun, she spent the rest of her days helping to build up the fledgling convent and embroidering vestments. There she died in 1857.

Afterword

The story of Doña Concha, her courtship by Count Rezanov, and her "second life" became very popular in the years after her death. In the second half of the 1800's, her story was celebrated throughout California in books, poems, songs, and legend.

To Fly with the Swallows is based on several of these sources. However, because these sources focus more on Concha's romance with Rezanov, routine details of her daily life are scarce. Where necessary we have drawn on accounts of everyday life in Spanish California to recreate Concha's daily life. Where reference is made to Concha's or Rezanov's thoughts or words, we have relied on what was reported in the stories and poems about them.

NOTES

Pages 3–4 A presidio was a military outpost. Yerba Buena was at the westernmost part of the Spanish Empire, more than five thousand miles from the seat of Spanish government. Alta (High) California comprised what we know today as California. Baja (Low) California is today one of the states of Mexico.

Page 5 Francis (1181?–1226) of Assisi, Italy, was a well-loved person who practiced gentleness and peacefulness in his daily life. Although born to a wealthy family, he gave up his riches and lived in poverty. He founded the Franciscan order of monks, who adopted his simple way of life and pledged themselves to helping the poor and the sick. Francis was especially well known for his loving compassion toward animals. Two years after his death, he was made a saint by the Roman Catholic Church.

Page 5 Many European countries, including Spain, Britain, France, and Russia, competed with one another to claim territory in the Americas. The British already had claims to much of what is now Canada, and the Russians had a settlement in what is now Alaska. The French had bought the huge Louisiana Territory from Spain and then had sold it to the United States. California was therefore bordered by territories claimed by foreign powers and was so far away from Spain that it was difficult to protect. One measure Spain took was to forbid trade between foreign governments and California.

Page 6 The eight-month overland journey to Mexico City from Yerba Buena covered a distance of about 1,800 miles. The length of time needed for the trip was due partly to the fact that there were only horses and horse-drawn vehicles available in 1806 and partly due to the bad roads and rough terrain.

In the early part of the nineteenth century, it was not at all unusual for young women to marry at fifteen or even earlier. This was in part because of the shorter life expectancy of the time, especially for women. In addition to being at risk from diseases and malnutrition, women faced the extra risk of death in childbirth. Although some people lived until seventy or older (Benjamin Franklin, for instance, lived to be eighty-four), the average life expectancy was around forty years.

Page 8 The padres—priests—were often the only people in a settlement like Yerba Buena who had any formal education. They would also be among the few who had any books. Priests would be responsible for the schooling of boys and young men. It was unusual for a girl to be given education outside the home.

Page 9 Houses in many parts of the Spanish Empire were built in the Spanish style, around a central patio or inner courtyard. This kept the house a little cooler in summer. In winter, it provided an outdoor area that was sheltered from cold winds.

Page 12 The British explorer George Vancouver visited Alta California in 1792. In 1791, Spain and Britain almost went to war over a dispute involving land in what is now western Canada. Vancouver was sent to North America by sea to try to avoid a fight. On his way, he explored and mapped much of the coastline along his route. Today, Vancouver Island, located off the Canadian coast, as well as two cities, bear his name.

Page 21 The Czar was the Emperor of Russia. Unlike Britain and Spain, Russia did not have much of an overseas empire; Alaska was their only North American colony, and they had no holdings in South America or among the Pacific Islands. But the land area of Russia was a giant expanse stretching across a large part of eastern Europe and all of northern Asia.

Page 25 Rezanov, like most Russian Christians of his time, belonged to the Russian Orthodox Church. Though the Roman Catholic Church (the church to which most people of the Spanish Empire belonged) and the Russian Orthodox Church are both Christian churches, they were and are independent of each other. In the early 1800's, it was unusual for people belonging to different religious groups to marry each other.

Page 32 For centuries, many Catholic men and women wishing to live an especially religious life have lived separately from the world in their own communities. They might come out into the world to teach, to tend the poor, or to work as healers. Concha would have liked to live the religious life, but there were no such communities for women in California until 1850.

Page 41 The first medicines were plants. Indeed, many modern medicines were first based on elements taken from plants. In Concha's day, when doctors were scarce, most people got what little medical treatment they could find from a neighbor who had studied the uses of local plants. More often than not, this neighbor was a woman. Thus, although women were not allowed into most medical schools until the 1840's, it can be said that women were in the medical profession since ancient times.

Page 42 There was no indoor plumbing system in the houses of the early 1800's. Water was drawn from a nearby stream, or an outdoor well was dug. In Alta California, the *aguador* was the person who carried water to the house.

Dana Catharine de Ruiz is a Spanish teacher and freelance writer. She lives in New York City with her sons, Mario Bernardo and Eduardo Felipe. Ms. Catharine de Ruiz is also the co-author of *La Causa The Migrant Farmworkers' Story.*